A Note to Parents and Teachers

Dorling Kindersley Readers is a compelling new reading programme for children, designed in conjunction with leading literacy experts, including Cliff Moon M.Ed., Honorary Fellow of the University of Reading. Cliff Moon has spent many years as a teacher and teacher educator specializing in reading and has written more than 140 books for children and teachers. He reviews regularly for teachers' journals.

Beautiful illustrations and superb full-colour photographs combine with engaging, easy-to-read stories to offer a fresh approach to each subject in the series. Each *Dorling Kindersley Reader* is guaranteed to capture a child's interest while developing his or her reading skills, general knowledge, and love of reading.

The four levels of *Dorling Kindersley Readers* are aimed at different reading abilities, enabling you to choose the books that are exactly right for each child:

Level 1 – Beginning to read
Level 2 – Beginning to read alone
Level 3 – Reading alone
Level 4 – Proficient readers

The "normal" age at which a child begins to read can be anywhere from three to eight years old, so these levels are intended only as a general guideline.

No matter which level you select, you can be sure that you are helping children learn to read, th read to learn!

www.dk.com

Editor Rachel Harrison
Art Editor Jane Horne

Senior Editor Linda Esposito
Senior Art Editor
Diane Thistlethwaite
Production Melanie Dowland
Picture Researcher Frances Vargo
Jacket Designer Victoria Harvey

Natural History Consultant
Theresa Greenaway
Reading Consultant
Cliff Moon M.Ed.

Published in Great Britain by
Dorling Kindersley Limited
9 Henrietta Street
London WC2E 8PS

2 4 6 8 10 9 7 5 3 1

A CIP catalogue record for this book is
available from the British Library.

ISBN 0-7513-2827-8

Colour reproduction by Colourscan, Singapore
Printed and bound in China by L. Rex Printing Co. Ltd.

The publisher would like to thank the following for
their kind permission to reproduce their photographs:
Key: a=above, c=centre, b=below, l=left, r=right, t=top

Aquila: Michael Edwards 4 inset, Anthony Cooper 29t; **Bruce Coler**
Collection: 4–5, 7b, 8, 9, 10t, 12–13, 16–17, 18–19, Andrew Purce
14–15, Jane Burton 20, Kim Taylor 22–23; **Dorling Kindersley**: Co
Keates 5 inset; **Natural History Photographic Agency**: E.A. Janes
Stephen Dalton 21r; **Oxford Scientific Films**: J.S. & E.J. Woolmer
Premaphotos Wildlife: 25, Ken Preston-Mafham 29c; **Richard Rev**
7t, 28–29; **RSPCA Photolibrary**: Jonathan Plant 6, E.A. Janes 30–
Windrush Photos: Dennis Green 24, Frank Blackburn 26–27

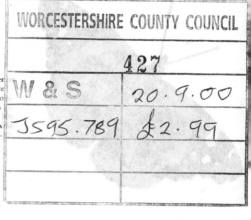

DK DORLING KINDERSLEY *READERS*

BEGINNING
1
TO READ

Born to Be a Butterfly

Written by Karen Wallace

DK

London • New York • Sydney • Delhi
Paris • Munich • Johannesburg

A butterfly flits
from flower to flower.
Her red-striped wings
shine in the sun.

wings

She touches the petals
with her feet and her feelers.

feelers

She looks for a leaf
where she can lay
her eggs.

A butterfly flits
from leaf to leaf.

On each little leaf
she lays one or two eggs.
She squeezes the eggs
out of her body.
The outside of each egg
is made of thin shell.

shell

A caterpillar grows inside each egg. Soon one is ready to hatch.

caterpillar

She bites through the shell
with her strong, sharp jaws.
She munches the leaves
around her.

The caterpillar makes
a tent from a leaf.

She hides from the birds,
who are sharp-eyed and hungry.

Hundreds of caterpillars
hatch alongside her.
Some are unlucky.
Hungry birds peck them.
Furry bats snatch them.
Spiders catch them.

The caterpillar is hungry.
She needs to grow, so
she crawls from her leaf tent.
She climbs up strong stems and
clings onto young leaves.

The caterpillar munches
and crunches
all the leaves she can find.

Munch!
Crunch!

The caterpillar munches
and crunches.
She gets bigger and bigger.
Her black and yellow skin
gets tighter and tighter.

skin

Suddenly the skin
starts to split open!
The caterpillar wriggles out
with a brand-new skin.

The caterpillar grows quickly.
She sheds her skin
four times before
she is fully grown.

She looks for
a leaf
that is sturdy
and strong.

She hangs upside down.

The caterpillar
is changing
into a chrysalis
(KRIS-uh-liss).

chrysalis

Outside,
her skin turns hard
to keep her safe.

Inside,
something amazing
is happening.

Then one day
the chrysalis splits open.
Something crawls out
into the sunshine.

legs

It has a head and six legs.
It has wings and a body.
Whatever can it be?

A brand-new butterfly
rests in the sunshine!
She is too wet to fly.

She holds out her wings
to help them dry faster.

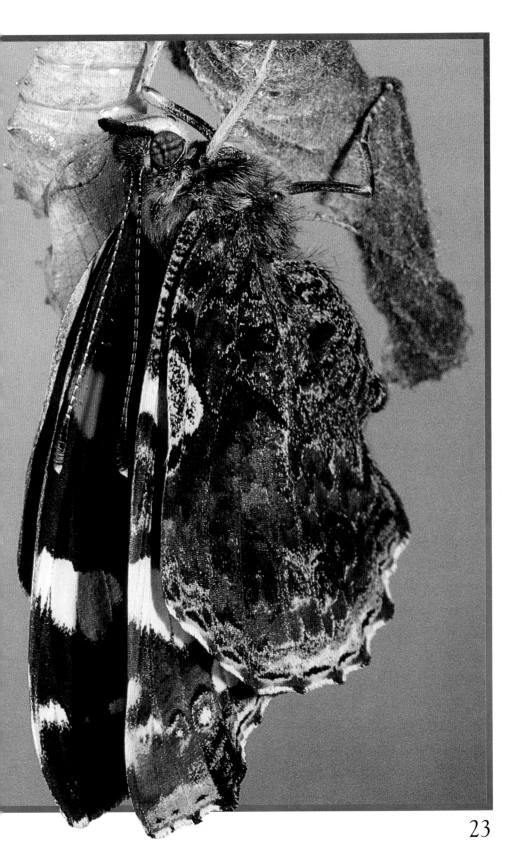

The butterfly flits
from flower to flower.
She sucks up the sweet nectar
with her long hollow tongue.
When she is not eating,
her tongue is curled
like a spring.

tongue

Sometimes she rests
with her wings held together.
She looks brown as the tree bark,
so hungry birds can't see her.

Now it is time
to look for a mate.
She finds him
sitting on a leaf.

They dance
in the sunshine and
fly off together.

The butterfly flits
from flower to flower.
Her red-striped wings
shine in the sun.

She looks for a leaf
where she can lay her eggs.

Soon, a hundred
more butterflies
will fly in the sun.

Picture Word List

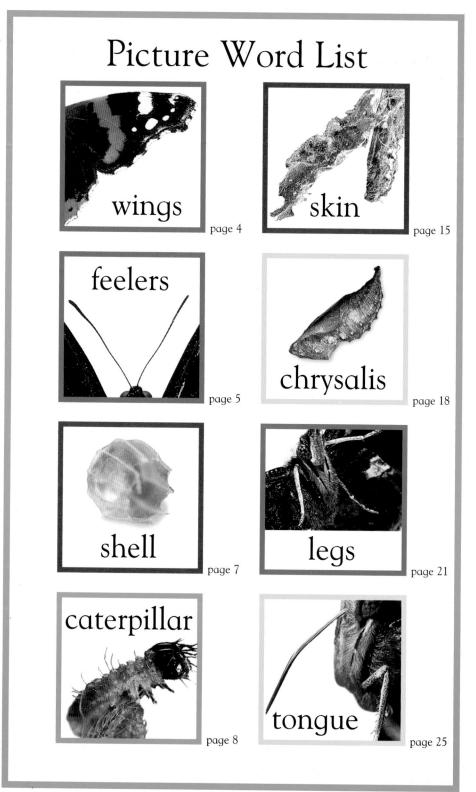

wings
page 4

skin
page 15

feelers
page 5

chrysalis
page 18

shell
page 7

legs
page 21

caterpillar
page 8

tongue
page 25